Lucent

Linda Ford

To Matt
Very best wishes.
Linda.

erbacce-press retain © copyright 2022 of this book
in its current format

Editing and typesetting © copyright 2022 Dr. Alan Corkish
Cover design © copyright 2022 Pascale Gouverneur based on a
photograph taken by Pascale in Gaudí's Casa Batlló in Barcelona

erbacce-press publications Liverpool UK 2022

www.erbacce-press.co.uk - scan below to visit

ISBN: 978-1-912455-35-5

Acknowledgements

Warm thanks to the editors of the following publications/organisations in which some of these poems (or earlier versions) were published. The High Window, Frosted Fire, Reach, Orbis, Southport Writers' Poetry Competition, Jewish Book Week, Daily Mirror, Diamond Twig, WEA, The Alchemy Spoon, Derbyshire Libraries, tiny wren lit.

Dedication

For my family, with love

Contents

What Keeps Us
Fern with beech roots and leaves, a watercolour by Kate Nessler.

Connectedness,
fronds of new fern,
carcasses of birch leaves riven
folded down the spine.
The brittleness of rust-brown tendrils,
lightening forks of root constellations
                  and the earth holding fast –

waiting for rain.

Growing Golden Oyster Mushrooms

Pent-up darkness,
the aroma of fusty air
and ancient woodland.
Fine strands, cotton balls,
as mycelium migrates
up through the substrate
impinging the light.
Yesterday small pins appeared
sensing their escape –
inflating where minute florets,
greyish-white nodules
turn antenna-like
their blind contortions
straining. Pale discs
now dimpled,
torn, as if a sudden
growth spurt
has overwhelmed them.

Notes towards the Oyster Mushroom
(Pleurotus ostreatus)
after Francis Ponge

Like a garland –
yellow-brown with whitish gills
and a lateral stalk.
Displays a tenacious attachment
to hardwoods
(fallen logs, dead trees).
Fleshy and large:
appends itself in a shelf-like
manner, being named for the shape
rather than taste.
The top notes are of fruit and anise,
which on cooking leave lingering
inferences of the sea.

Barn Fire

In a bid to save the barn
they stemmed the river;
as the water ebbed,
we climbed down into

the cavernous riverbed,
explored the unread world
of weed-wrapped pebbles
and mysterious detritus.

Later, as the dam was
released, we saw how fast
the river flowed, how soon
our footprints disappeared.

The Brook

tarries before joining the river
pebbles clink as they collide in shallows,
toes cramp and shale carves into feet
but they are lustrous, and we long to hold them.
Chosen ones stuffed into pockets or tossed
aground to dry, where they become washed-out,
submissive. We return them to the water

as the sun casts a long shadow.

Spring Mycena

There is an unseemliness
about decayed wood,
a sadness – a slow forgetting.
Those who gain
from that which flakes and crumbles
proliferate in what remains of life.
I map your spore print
crossveins:
radial striations.

Buddleja

And I have seen the changes,
clocked the fractured light

that breaks across the stone,
the fretfulness of bees

each passing cloud and sound –
a single pearl of rain,

the faintest breath of wings,
each faded bud and leaf.

Listen to the birdsong
muted by the wind.

You Can Feel

Corn, a watercolour by Kate Nessler.

the imminence of rain
a weight of cloud upon the air

and paint upon the page,
kernels withered in their skins

an unmade bed of leaves:
this picture is about waiting.

The Art of Chinese Brush Painting

With a solitary goat-hair,
each stroke brings forth
the essence of a lotus flower.

Camanchaca

From the lip of the coast –
a mist on the Atacama
awakens seeds from dunes,
where desert miles become fields
of mallow flowers.

Notes:
Camanchaca means creeping fog in Spanish.
The Atacama Desert is in Chile.

Lichen

When you reach
the forest
regard fernlike fronds
and barnacles
of amber-russet.

Let fingertips disturb
trails of liver spot,
seaweed marooned
as each spore breaks rank:
sails its name on the air.

Violet Coral Fungus *(Clavaria zollingeri)*

The   ground   is   broadleaved
and   coniferous
    as   each   magenta   tentacle
    hesitantly
tries   the   air

Grandmother Cooking Mushrooms

She cooked slowly
with both love and precision,
each specimen dismembered

as part of an intricate ritual,
releasing flavour and aroma
before she watched us eat –

her vicarious pleasure
as we devoured
something she could not.

Lassithi Plateau *(Crete)*

There is something reassuring
about the insomnia of turbines,
like the circularity of a clock's
inner workings. As each gyration
fully realised, is then negated
by the next and so on, as though
if you stare too long, you might
lose yourself.

21

Wasp's Nest
Homage to Jane Kenyon.

A wasp has made her nest
inside the padlock
by the door. I imagine
the writhe of larvae
in the mechanism, and watch
as she repeatedly
approaches the keyhole,
then hesitates
as if unable to cross
even her own threshold.

Kite

Lofty as the wind chooses,
billowing wash days,
feral horses riding the
bridle line.

Gregarious as a yacht's sails,
ripples up the tail,
paper chains
and Rapunzel's tresses.

To wrestle ascent
with zip, zip, zither,
spool-decanting line-hooking
fish-into-the-air.

The Major Oak *(Edwinstowe)*

The silence is immutable,
as you lean towards me

I am welcomed
like an old friend.

Clouds that came and went
are now forgotten,

as leaves are torn
or left to harden on the branch.

You seem diminished –
I thought I knew you.

Japanese Knotweed

These hurts have seeded
far downstream
(and I did not see them coming).

On the riverbank, meadowsweet
have raised
their white flags –

fibrous roots allow little
resistance: just an urge
to grow and grow.

Bulrushes

The bulrushes are poised:
half-turned to seed,
dithering somewhere
between duck-down and velveteen.

Pennytown

The carp lie silent
in the shallows,
their shadows rarely

seen, even in the margins.
But look – a fish
has breached,

watch its silvered arc:
how it schillers
in the light.

Carp Sex

the carp
are spawning,
they thrash and twist

in the reed beds.
afterwards,
the water

is awash
with the glut
     of eggs and milt.

The Truth About Honesty *(lunaria)*

So clear yet still opaque –
flower and fruit so dissimilar

where seeds drift on peripherals
and each translucent disk promises an ocean.

Like knowing everything has changed:
this futile clinging to the shore.

Flannan Isle

Nights are long
at Eilean Mòr Lighthouse
west coast.
Sometimes on inclement
nights shouts are heard,
a roll-call over the dark swell.
Mac Arthur, Ducat, Marshall

names filling gullies,
swallowed by an ink-black sway.
Pay no heed to siren calls
but batten down the hatches –
pray that sea-madness will pass
surely as tides carry the waves.
God is over all.

After the Storm

Along the coastal path,
there is evidence

of the night's storm:
leaves and kindling

brushed aside, patches
of the earth exposed –

amidst the chaos,
nothing is forgotten.

Seashell

Before you were sea-wrapped
each recollection   hidden
between lip and pinnacle

involute
cavern-like whorls
gregarious as mountain ranges

footholds fade
ribbed against   the turned sand
barnacled

f r a g m e n t e d   in your hand
listen
clutch this shell

tight   against   your   ear
close enough to hear
the anthem

of   soft,   slow   waves
always undeterred
always something taken

from the shore

Daffodils

I'm taken with the daffodils,
the way their heads seek out
the light: skin-like spathes
from which the perianth appears;
each flower singled out –
a tubular crown, toothed, where the gold
is more profound: how every glaucous
leaf enlarges after flowering.

Honeybee

This small ball of velveteen
in the palette of Van Gogh
was barely moving. Cupped
in my hand, he sipped
the proffered sugared water –
I witnessed his revival.

Vincent's Flowers
Van Gogh, *Sunflowers* (1889)

Was the sunflower
conceived just for you?
amongst those gilded landscapes –
that bee-bright sway.

Wolf Lichen *(Letharia volpina)*

Imagine a forest devoid
of branches, so dense
you might lose your way,
a coral reef without the sea –
this surge of lichen
by the deadwood:
by the stream.

From Acorns

Just wide of the oak's
reach, acorns once
buried and forgotten,
form oaklet clusters
which sprout in the loam.
Neighbouring trees
have been haloed, allowing
the oak to receive more light.
Only when the rootstocks
are strong, do saplings
declare themselves
above ground.

Green Man

There is a fusion of wild
foliate, which intertwines
with oak and hawthorn.
He speaks in cascades
of green-leafed garland.

Airborne

She leaps –
gill-plates wide
a rush of air

as those un-blinkered
eyes perceive
our airborne world.

Acanthus No: 35
W. Morris design for *Acanthus Wallpaper (*1874*)*

As leaves fade to golden, blackberries
obscured by a festoon of leaves

their galaxy of soft warm fruitfulness
apparent only by their shine.

The pattern repeats –
sometimes it's hard to look away.

The Pearls and the Paste
A photograph of Carolina Otero was
taken in 1954 by Edward Quinn.

The balcony –

awash

with breadcrumb

and seed,

scattered like the husks

of old lovers

and still, *pigeonnes* fly

above the city.

About Balloons

Comprised of
almost nothing
stretched between air –

string's rock and hum
upended pendulum;

tight as a Kilner
taught as a harp-string
light as a shadow

… almost nothing.

The Ways of Light

Fragments are sized, anchored,
and oiled by steady hands,
a knotted heart elongates –
the map of long slow grain
reaches out across the afternoon,
where all that matters is the alchemy
of light and shadow, its path
across the mellowed wood.

5 a.m.

Sometimes when rain scripts
its tributaries and beckons
on the glass, birds hide

under leafed canopies, seek comfort
in each other, huddled together,
eager for the night to pass.

By the window, a cappuccino
cold, stale beneath its skin
it's dawn outside - a chorus begins.

The Alchemy of Clouds

Cirrus, Cumulus, Stratus
a triptych of clouds set adrift
across a green-belt sky.

*Luke Howard named varieties of cloud in 1802.

Spring Forest

The   spring   wends
its   way   into
the   heartbeat
of   the   forest.
As   each   leaf   unfurls,
a   lime-green   clutch
of   new   growth   carpets
the   canopy.
Crowned   by   delicate
sunlight,   each   season is   sanguine,
follows   its   ancestors
into   the   headlights.

Lighting the Lanterns
Carnation, Lily, Lily, Rose.
by John Singer-Sargent (1885-6).

Paper lanterns –
strung out
like musical scores.

The children are intent:
illuminating each orb in turn
as their faces take on the light.

Fireflies

amongst the bracken
blue lights emit their signal –
blink in unison

Cemetery Gates

Cemetery Gates a painting
by Casper David Freidrich (1825)

They have seen you
turned towards the tooth stones
where breath might
fold you away –
as sentinel trees
carve silhouette rivers
into half-dark,
half-light.

Drystone Wall

Cross each joint, one-stone-
on-two, two-stones-on-one,
set them down, best-face up.
              Pack the spaces tight
with *hearting* stones: *through*
stones hold it all together –
how each stone plays its part,
knows its place.

Pressing Flowers

Six weeks ahead of us,
loud as a buttercup meadow
>
>we contrive crop circles in the grass,
>
>pick anemone and foxglove,
>
>kingcup and toadflax –
>
>as if naming each flower
might invoke their spirit.
>
>As we lay them out across the pages,
some leaves are tightly held:
sticky with past pressings.

Pebbles

Over time, you will forget
the bluish-rustic tones,

as hands explore the scores
and weathered lines, but understand

that although vibrancies will fade,
every pebble is equal.

Sea Dance

Sometimes when the storm
has passed, the surf
releases glass,
kelly-green, amberina
rolling in the long-
shore drift.

Aurora Borealis

Aurora - goddess of the dawn.
Stars are undiminished
through the luminosity,
where arcs of light pulsate
in hues of ammolite:
scarlet, carmine, green.

Outcrop

The landscape is smooth, unfamiliar
after the earthmover has washed its face.
Harebell and orchid have dwindled,
the storm-felled oak no longer straddles
the brook, and the cottage (where we played)
is now a ruin. With eyes closed, I listen:
the sounds remain.

Nocturne

The Starry Night.
Painting by Vincent Van Gogh (1889)

The sky has mounted a coup
on the landscape, and the sun
gives no amnesty when all
you see is darkness.
Cloudbanks trip into the vale,
as cobalt gives birth
to orbs of light.

Love Locks *(On the Bridge)*

The signs were clear
but still, they came,
initials intertwined
with ribbon.
A girl who can't
be more than sixteen
looks heartbroken,
but seems compelled
to leave an offering.
I heard a piece
of *Pont des Arts*
bridge collapsed
in Paris; as if unable
to withstand the weight
of all that love.

Kulnura *(New South Wales)*

This place of charcoal trees
where sequoias rise –
grow tall, look towards the sea.

Note:
Kulnura means; *in sight of the sea.*

The Sacrifice

I hear their incantations
as they encircle open water
and light forces itself
through the canopy.
From the bridge,
there's a glimpse of crimson
and feather –
stark against the mariposa.

Last Day

And it was just as if the weight
of our hearts had been felt

in the concaves of our footprints,
as if we might revolt

against the half-toppled cairns:
as if we might refuse to leave.

About the author

Linda Ford originates from a therapeutic background and (when she isn't writing) works in the charity sector.

She holds an M.A. in Creative Writing (Distinction) from the Open University and was a 2021 recipient of the *Genesis Jewish Book Week Emerging Writers' Programme.*

Her poetry has been published in various literary journals and has been placed, shortlisted or longlisted in a number of competitions, including *Frosted Fire Firsts, Southport Writers'* and *Buzzwords poetry competitions.*

She lives in Derbyshire with her husband and grown-up children. You can visit her personal website via the QR code below: